STEP ONE:

Play **Piano**

by Ernest Lubin
**Master the basics of hand position, note reading, scales, melody,
and chords as you step into the exciting world of piano playing.
A complete guide to getting a good start at the piano.**

Cover photography by Randall Wallace

This book Copyright © 1997 by Amsco Publications,
A Division of Music Sales Corporation, New York

Order No. AM 943162
US International Standard Book Number: 0.8256.1610.7
UK International Standard Book Number: 0.7119.6480.7

Exclusive Distributors:
Music Sales Corporation
257 Park Avenue South, New York, NY 10010 USA
Music Sales Limited
8/9 Frith Street, London W1V 5TZ England
Music Sales Pty. Limited
120 Rothschild Street, Rosebery, Sydney, NSW 2018, Australia

Printed in the United States of America by
Vicks Lithograph and Printing Corporation

Amsco Publications
New York/London/Sydney

CD Track List

Bonus Tracks—instrumental backup for practice or performance:

Contents

Preliminaries

How many of us have dreamed of learning to play the piano, and put it off because we felt it might be too difficult. Well, it is difficult, particularly to play well. But it's not impossible. Certainly, it's not difficult to make a start. In fact, most of us have been near enough to a piano to make something of a start on our own, and if we had a good ear, we may have accomplished more than we realize.

While this book cannot pretend to make a pianist out of you—for that you need a teacher and some hard work—it can help you to make a start, and it can help teach you a little about the piano until you find a teacher. And perhaps it may make you a little better prepared when you do start lessons.

In the meantime, however, don't be afraid of the piano. You may do many things wrong, but you may even do some things right. Let us begin, by walking to the piano and playing a note or two. Can you play "Chopsticks"? Or can you pick up a simple tune by ear? Well, that's a beginning, and we may be able to build from there.

Let us first become acquainted with a few necessary technicalities. We will have to learn the names of the notes for one thing. And we will have to learn the names of the fingers from a pianist's point of view. That at least is very simple— they are numbered from one to five beginning with the thumb, and the little numbers above (or below) the notes in piano music show what finger you have to play the note with.

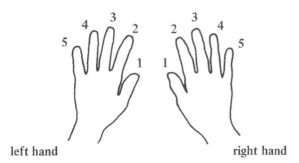

left hand   right hand

And then too we will have to learn how long to hold the notes. That's very important, too, but we shall put it off until the next chapter, since we simply can't start with everything at once.

The Keyboard

Now let us take another look at the piano. Some notes are white and some are black, and you will notice that the black notes are arranged in groups of twos and threes. It will be easier to start playing with the white notes, but we have to identify them in relation to the black notes. The white note between the two black notes is called "D," and if you count them you will see that there are seven Ds on the piano altogether.

Let us take the D nearest the middle of the piano, under the piano maker's name. That is "middle" D, and the next white note below it is middle C. Going down two more steps we find B and A, and going up from D we have E, F, and G. Then we start a new series with A again.

To return to the middle C, which we shall use as our starting point at the piano—put the thumb of your right hand on middle C and play it. And now, with your thumb resting over C, place one finger over each successive note without skipping any. This bring you up to G. Now beginning with C, play all five notes slowly, one after another. Then play G again, and play the same notes going down. This will be our first exercise, and we shall see how it looks in music notation.

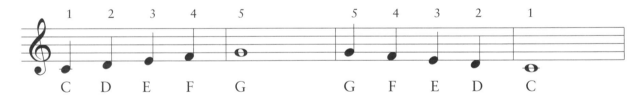

Now you have taken your first step toward becoming a pianist, but there is a good deal to think about before going further. For example, some positions of the hand are easier to work with than others, and naturally it will be a good idea to get into the habit of using a good hand position.

A Note on Hand Position

Look at the photo on the top of page 7. This represents a normal and correct position of the hand at the piano. You will notice that the fingers are curved and that the top of the finger plays a note by falling directly from above. This is the most important single detail to remember about your hand position, for the commonest mistake that beginners make is to play with the fingers flat.

correct hand position

Here below is a picture of what *not* to do! It's possible to play the piano like that, but it's difficult and ungainly, and you won't get very far that way.

incorrect position

One other detail that is important to remember: Keep the wrist fairly low, about on a level with the keys. Thus the hand will be slightly arched, with the highest point at the knuckles. Positively it may help at the beginning to imagine that you are holding a small object in the hollow of your hand as you play, and you can even make the experiment of stuffing a very small wad of paper into the hollow of your hand, and playing a note or two without letting it drop. This may help curve the hand. Don't try this too long, though, for it may make the hand a little tense, and you'll get the best results at the piano by being as relaxed as you can (while, of course, keeping a good hand position).

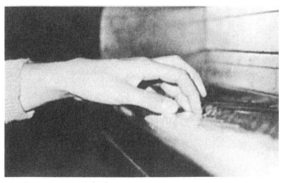

wrist evenwith keys

This will all take a little time and practice. Don't become discouraged if you can't attain an ideal hand position at the beginning. Just do the best you can, and keep on playing. You may find it helpful to observe the hand position of other pianists as they play. Perhaps you can get to a concert, or catch a pianist on TV, or you may have friends who play the piano well. Incidentally, there is no one precise position that applies to every hand. Each pianist tends to find his own way of playing within the framework of a normal position at the piano.

Now that we have spent a little time discussing hand position, try that exercise we did at first, but this time do it with as good a hand position as you can.

Here is the exercise again.

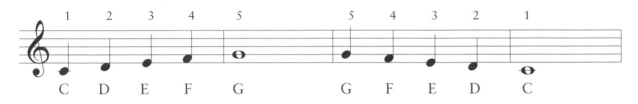

Notice, by the way, that the fingers should be directly above the keys, but not actually touching them except for the key that is being played. Another common mistake that beginners make is to let their fingers fly in the air in all directions when the are not playing a note. Here is another photo of what to avoid!

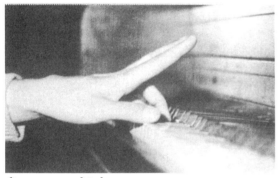

fingers too high

Of course you will have to play this exercise rather slowly if you are going to remember all the things we said about hand position, but it is good to play slowly when you are practicing. Later on it will be easy enough to play as fast as you want.

Now that you have played this exercise with the right hand, try it with the left an octave lower. That is, begin with the left hand on the first C that you come to below middle C, and start with the fifth finger.

Here is how the left hand looks in music notation.

(bass clef)

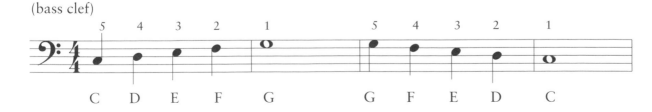

In order to write notes in the lower range. for the left hand, we need a
different clef. For the right hand we have used the *treble clef* or *G clef* (&), so
named because it circles the line on which G above middle C is written. For the
left hand we will use the *bass clef* or *F clef* (𝄢) which brackets the line on which
F below middle C is written.

If you've practiced these exercises even as much as a few minutes with each
hand, that's enough for now. There's a limit to how long you can practice an
exercise like this without getting tired. But when you can do it fairly well, and
would like something more difficult, then play both hands together an octave
apart, and so evenly that they sound like one. That's more difficult than you
think, but you can try it, and it will give you something to aim for as you keep
practicing.

both hands together:

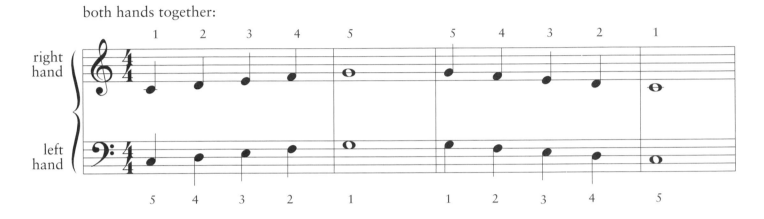

As you play this exercise, hold each note until you have sounded the next
note, and then let it go. This smooth joining of notes is called *legato,* and is
normally used for most of the music you play. The opposite is called *staccato,*
and means that the notes are played sharply and separated from each other.

We will soon be taking up a great many new and more difficult things, but
this little five-finger exercise will be useful for a long time in developing a good
hand position and in acquiring facility at the piano. Keep practicing it every day
for a few moments as a warming up exercise in each hand and in both hands
together before you go on to anything else.

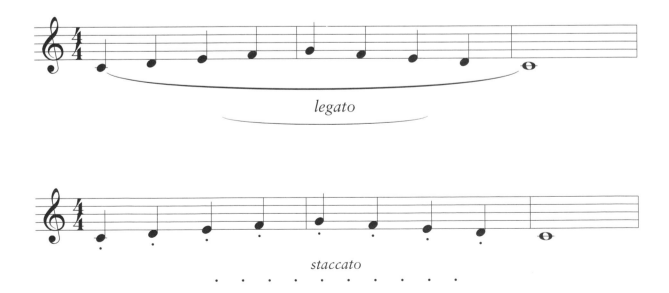

Music Notation

In the first lesson we saw how our finger exercise looked in music notation, and you will notice that music notation is a simple and logical system. It's much easier to pick up than, for example, the alphabet, which we all learned easily enough as children. When the notes go up the music goes up, and when the notes go down the music goes down, and as you will observe, each successive line and space stands for a successive musical pitch.

Since we have started with middle C, let us look at it again in music notation. here, first, is where the note is on the keyboard,

and here it is in music notation. Look at it, and then play it.

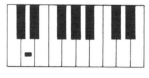

The next note going up, D, looks like this. Play this one too.

Then comes E, which looks like this. Play it.

Now let us come back to C once more, and play it again.

These four notes together, one after another, form the beginning of the familiar French folk song, "Frère Jacques," and here is how they look in music notation.

barline

Try playing these four notes one after another very steadily and evenly. They make up a musical unit known as a bar or measure. marking the end of the bar is a straight line called the *barline*.

If you sing "Frère Jacques" you will notice that the first bar is repeated. Try playing it twice; here is how it is written.

Going ahead with the next measure of this tune, you will see that it has only three notes, but that the last note is held twice as long as the others. Try this at the piano; here is how it looks.

To indicate that the last note is held twice as long as the others, a slightly different note is used, with its head outlined instead of being filled in. This kind of note is called a *half note* while the others are called *quarter notes*.

The easiest way of learning to play notes of different lengths correctly is to count in terms of quarter notes, holding each quarter note for one count, and each half note for two counts, while counting four beats to a measure. If we go back to "Frère Jacques" again, it will provide us with a simple illustration of how to count. Here are the first four bars of "Frère Jacques" in music notation.

Frè - re Jacqu - es,   Frè - re Jacqu - es,   dor - mez vous?   dor - mez vous?

Try playing it and singing the words, while following the music notation
with your eyes at the same time.

Now do it again, but instead of singing the words, sing the counts of the
measure as follows.

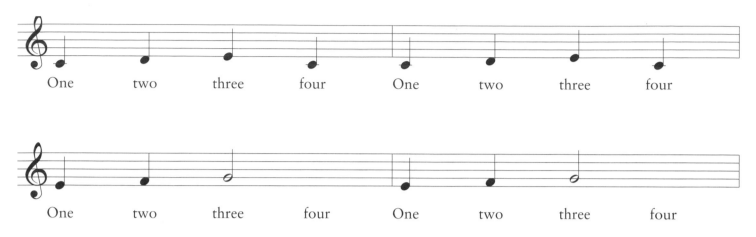

In the last two measures be sure to count the third and fourth beats while
you hold the note G. Remember that once you start to count, you must continue
to count the beats evenly without stopping. You can hold a note longer, but you
can't hold a beat longer. In a way, the fundamental beat that you establish in
music might be compared to the heartbeat, which keeps going steadily whether
you are moving slower or faster.

Of course, the notes of the music can move faster as well as slower than the
beat. The continuation of "Frère Jacques" is a good example of that, for in the
next measures the first four notes move twice as fast as quarter beats. Notes of
this type are called eighth notes and look like this.

Now here is the entire melody of "Frère Jacques" in music notation, and you
will see how the eighth notes fit into the pattern of the measure.

One   two   three   four   One   two   three   four

One   two   three   four   One   two   three   four

The second part of the melody is a little harder to play at the piano than the first, since the range moves beyond the five notes that we have been working with so far, and you don't have to feel that it's necessary to be able to play it at the piano just yet. If you want to try it, go ahead—but you will have to adjust the fingering. At the beginning of the fifth and seventh measures, shift your hand position by using the fingering indicated below.

America

In case you've been wondering about the two numbers ($\frac{4}{4}$) at the beginning of "Frère Jacques," that's called the *time signature*. The top number indicates that there are four beats in each measure, and the bottom number indicates that each beat is a quarter note.

Often measures can be counted in threes. Does any example come to mind? If you thought of the "Blue Danube Waltz," you're right of course, for every waltz is counted in threes. In this case, the slight accent which falls on the first beat of every measure occurs every three counts, instead of every four counts as in "Frére Jacques."

Both our national anthems, "America" and the "Star-Spangled Banner," are in three-four time.*

Since "America" is the simpler of the two let us try it as our first piano piece in three-four time. This melody has a range of only five notes in its first part which will make it relatively easy to play at the piano. However, although the music starts on middle C the lowest note is going to be one note lower, B. Therefore let us begin on middle C. with the second finger so that the thumb will be free to play B when it appears. Try it by ear and see if you can get it. Here it is in music notation.

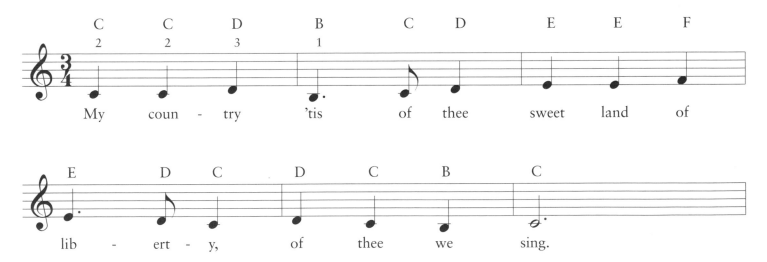

* You might like to notice an interesting difference rhythmically between these two anthems although they are both in time, "America" starts on the first beat of the measure while "The Star Spangled Banner" begins with an upbeat, that is on a weak beat before the beginning of the first full measure. If you sing them with the words, the difference will become clear "My country, 'tis of thee" obviously starts on a strong beat, while "Oh, say can you see" begins with a weak beat that leads into the strong beat on "say." Musical compositions are about equally divided into those that start with a downbeat and those that start with an upbeat, and is a good way of testing your ear and your sense of rhythm to see if you can tell the difference as you listen to a piece of music. There is a very close analogy to poetical metre, where "dactylic" lines start with a downbeat, and "iambic" lines start with an upbeat.

As you notice, it is in six measures of three-four time. There is all eighth note in the second measure, and another in the fourth measure, and since each measure has to have three full beats, we will hold the first quarter note of these measures a little longer to round out the three beats. This is indicated musically by adding a dot after these quarter notes, and you will see a dot used this way quite frequently. Technically, a dot after a note means that you extend it by half again its own length. Therefore, when you add a dot after a quarter note, it means that you have extended it by half of itself, or an eighth note; and when you add a dot after a half note, it means that you have extended it by half of itself, or in this case a quarter note. Thus a *dotted half note* is equal in counts to a half plus a quarter note, or three quarter notes. The last measure of our phrase of "America" is a dotted half note, which must be counted for three beats.

Now try playing "America" while counting, out loud, the three quarter beats in the measure. It's a little tricky due to the dotted quarter notes in measures two and four—they are held while you count one and two, and the eighth note comes in just before you count three. But if you count evenly and steadily and play the tune correctly in time, you may be able to get it. Here it is again in music notation, with the counts written in where they occur.

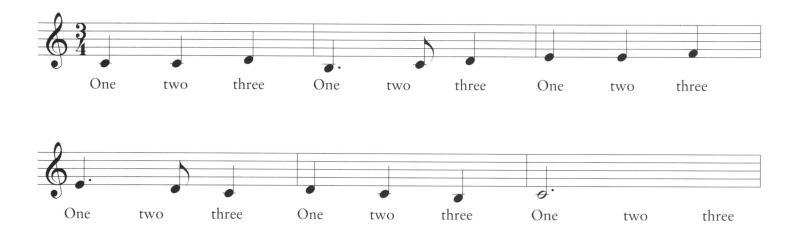

The second, fourth, and sixth measures of the piece could also have been written as follows.

The little curved line underneath the second and fourth and sixth measures is called a *tie,* and it means that you hold the second of the two connected notes without playing it again. Very likely the notation might be clearer that way, but the abbreviation of a dot after a note to indicate its being held for an extra half of its own length is used whenever possible, and we might as well get to know it!

Suggestions for Practice

At this stage you can hardly practice very long at a time—even ten or fifteen minutes is quite enough to spend on the material we have had so far. But do get into the habit of practicing consistently every single day. If you really want to learn to play the piano, this is the only way you can do it!

Begin each practice session with the five-finger exercise we had in the beginning. Work on it slowly and carefully and watch your hand position. Do it with each hand separately first, and then try it with hands together a little more slowly. Later on you can vary it occasionally by speeding it up a little, while still being careful to keep a good hand position.

Then work a little each day on the new piece of this lesson, "America," until you can get to play it quite easily and naturally.

Don't forget to give some time at each practice session to reviewing your old pieces. So far we only have one old piece that we can review, "Frère Jacques," but go over it as conscientiously as your new piece. The fifth and sixth measures of "Frère Jacques" are the most difficult, so practice them by themselves sometimes until they come to you as easily as the rest of the piece.

A Little Extra Practice

By now we have covered quite a good bit of ground, and before taking up anything new it might be helpful to apply what we have already learned to some other melodies.

Since we began with "Frère Jacques," here is another very charming French folksong, the first part of which is within the range of a few notes and uses simple rhythms.

Can you recognize it from looking at the music? If not, it is "Au Clair de la Lune," which you are likely know. This piece is in four-four time and begins with the thumb on middle C. As you notice, the first measure consists of four quarter notes, while the second measure has only two half notes. But since each half note is counted for two beats, these two notes are equivalent in time to the four quarter notes. The third measure is made up of four quarter notes again, while the last measure has one long note of four beats, which fills up the entire measure. This kind of note is called a *whole note* (○).

Play it again, counting the beats out loud. This is always good practice for learning to play in time.

Notice that these four bars are repeated. That is what the double bar with two dots at the end of the last measure indicates. It is called a *repeat sign*, and is often used to save space.

Would you like to play the next section of "Au Clair de la Lune"? Luckily, it has a range of only five notes, but since the notes are lower, going down to G below middle C, we will have to change the position of our hand and start this phrase on D with the fifth finger. Here it is in music notation.

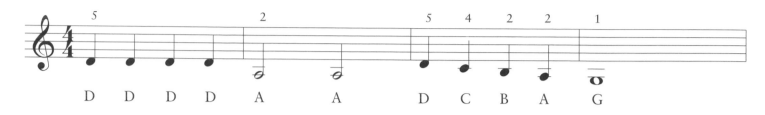

If you prefer you can play these same notes with the left hand beginning with the thumb. Here is how it looks written in the bass clef for the left hand.

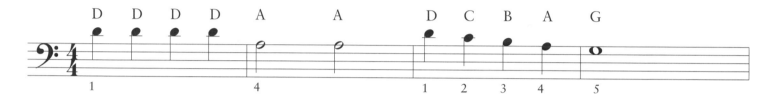

After you have played this middle section, go back to the first part and play it again to finish the piece.

Now here is another melody that we should be able to work out using the knowledge we have acquired. Start this one with the third finger on E.

This piece, as you notice, also has a repeat sign at the end, and the lines above the music with the numbers 1 and 2 underneath them mean that the two bars under figure 1 are played the first time around, and on the repeat you omit them and go directly to the two bars under figure 2.

This melody is somewhat more complicated rhythmically than "Au Clair de la Lune," but since it only uses the material we have taken up so far, you should be able to learn it with a little practice. Of course, it's the familiar refrain of "Jingle Bells," and you can probably play it by ear in case you have trouble reading the music. But in this case, go back to the printed music, and follow it with your eyes as you play it. This will help you familiarize yourself with music notation.

If later on you want to play this piece faster, go ahead and do so. You can count the beats at any speed you want, as long as you count them steadily once you establish the speed, or *tempo*.

Sight Reading

Since it is so important to be able to read music, let us try a little practice now in reading notes, purely as an exercise in sight reading. These exercises are now not based on familiar melodies, since that may become something of a crutch to lean on, and we must learn to get along without it.

Here, then, are some new melodies that fall within the range of a five-finger position. Start the first one with the thumb on middle C.

C   D   E   D   E   F

At first it may be easier to learn a new melody like this by figuring out the notes first, and saving the rhythmical problems until later. If you wish you may write the notes in letters below the musical notes, as we have done with the first two measures, but this of course is another crutch that you will learn to discard before long. After you are acquainted with the notes, do it in correct time, remembering to count the half notes for two counts, always counting the beats evenly.

One   two   three   four   One   two   three   four   *etc.*

Try this rhythmical variation of the first two measures, as always counting very steadily while you play.

One   two   three   four   One   two   three   four

Here is still another rhythmical variation of the first two measures. This particular rhythmic pattern occurs less frequently, but it is good practice too.

One   two   three   four   One   two   three   four

Eventually it will become second nature to distinguish between quarter notes, half notes, and dotted half notes, and later you will be able to dispense with counting out loud. But right now it is a good idea to bend over backwards to be correct rhythmically, since good rhythm is a basic requirement of good musicianship. If you have any doubts at all about the rhythm, count out loud! You can even tap your foot in time to the beat if you'd like—anything that will help you keep in time is worth doing!

Now let us practice a little in three-four time. In the next study all the notes are quarters except for the two dotted half notes, which are held for three counts. Again, learn the notes first, and then count it very steadily in threes.

Here are a few more exercises for rhythm. The first is entirely on middle C.

The next is in three-four time and is not difficult, but continue to count out loud as you play it, once you have learned the notes. Start this one with the fifth finger on G.

Would you like to try a little creative work yourself? If so, finish the next two melodies on your own, adding the missing four bars at the end of each piece.

The first one is in two-four time, which has only two beats to a measure, so you will need very few notes to complete the eight bars.

Now try one in three-four time.

As you will discover, it is really not too difficult to invent melodies. Don't just play them at the piano, however; write them out too.

Suggestions for Practice

Now that you are learning to read notes, it is important to get all the practice you can in sight reading. If you have any other beginner's book at home, look over the first pieces in it, and see how well you can read them. Feel free at this stage to write in the letters of the notes above the music, if you find it helpful.

Always remember that the rhythm is just as important as the notes. Often it is a good idea to practice the rhythmical patterns by themselves. You can tap your foot in time to the beats as you count them out loud, while clapping the rhythmical pattern, or playing it on one note. When you are sure of the rhythm, then apply it to the notes of the piece.

Of course, writing your own music is an excellent way of practicing the notes. In case you do the creative exercises in this lesson, then carefully write out what you have composed and practice your own music along with the other pieces you are learning.

Chords

While most of the melodies we have had so far mainly move stepwise— that is, from one note to its neighboring one—there are also many melodies that are based on skips. The beginning of "The Star Spangled Banner" is a typical example.

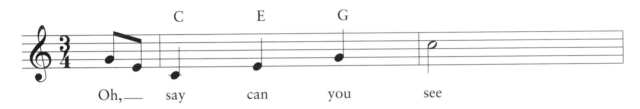

If you take the three notes of the first full measure, C, E, and G, and play them at the same time, you will find that they sound quite well together.

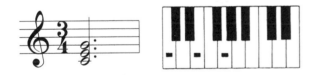

This happens to be one of the most commonly used chords in music, and if you want to be technical about it, you can call it the *tonic chord*, or the I (one) chord in C, or the *C Major chord*.

The notes of this chord often turn up in other melodies. Here's another example in "Sweet Betsy from Pike."

As you can see, the notes of the first measure again make up the C Major chord. If you try playing the three notes of the second measure together (G, F, and D), you will find that they too form a chord.

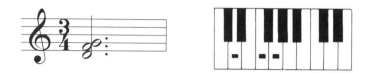

This is also a very commonly used chord; it is one of the positions of the dominant seventh chord, or the five seven chord (written V7).

These two chords, the I and V7 are so important and so useful that you will find it well worth the trouble of getting to know them. Play them a few times, one after another, in the right hand.

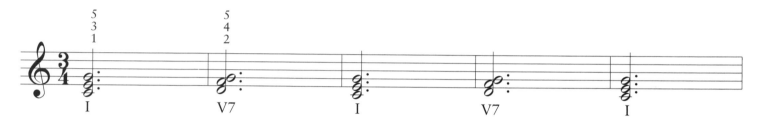

And now, to become even more familiar with them, try playing them in the left hand an octave lower (that is, start with the C, E, and G below middle C).

Now, try these chords in both hands together. (This may not be too easy at first, but you'll get it with a little practice.)

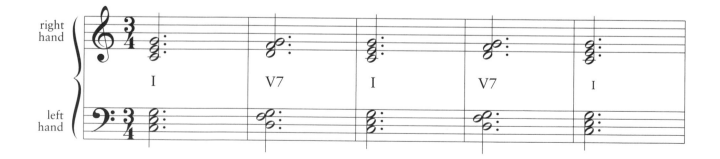

With these two chords alone it is now possible to harmonize a great many melodies. Since we usually play the melody in the right hand and the accompaniment in the left, review the chords once more in the left hand, and then we will put a melody on top of them.

Can you still play the melody of "America" that we had in the last lesson? Review it in the right hand, and then try playing it together with the I and the V7 chords as follows.

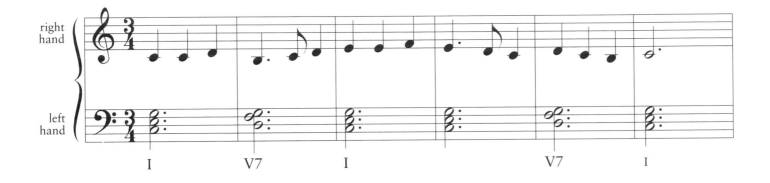

The rest of "America" can be harmonized with these two chords.

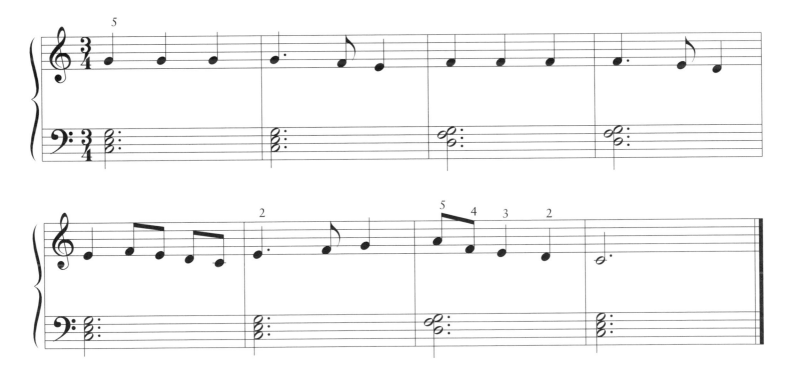

However, it does not fit ideally; the measure before the last is quite frankly a makeshift. We will have to learn a number of new chords, as well as new positions of the I and V7 chords before we can harmonize melodies just as we might wish. At this stage we are something like a person who knows pidgin English—our abilities are rather limited, but at least we can get along a little.

A Few Simple Pieces

Now that we know two chords, let us see if we can make up a few simple pieces based on them. Perhaps you may even find that you can invent melodies yourself to go along with them. Here is one possibility.

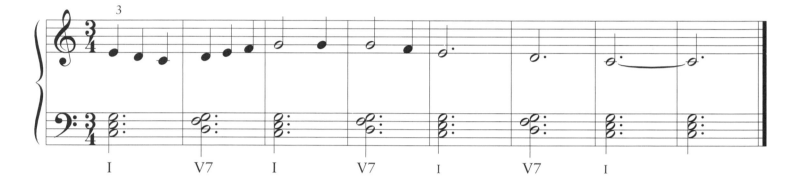

Notice the tie connecting the right-hand notes in the last two measures. That means you hold them continuously for their combined length, or six counts in all, while repeating the left-hand chords which are not tied.

Here is another melody based on our two chords. It is a little more difficult than the first because its range is seven notes instead of five, and that will mean adjusting the fingering to include the notes below middle C that occur in the second and seventh measures. But you may find you can handle it if you practice the melody alone at first. Start by learning the notes, and writing them in above the staff yourself if you find that helpful. After you have learned the notes, play them in correct time, counting out loud if necessary.

That little crossed note at the beginning of the seventh measure is called a
grace note (♪), and it means that you can play it in your own time before the
regular note which it precedes, making it as short as you wish.

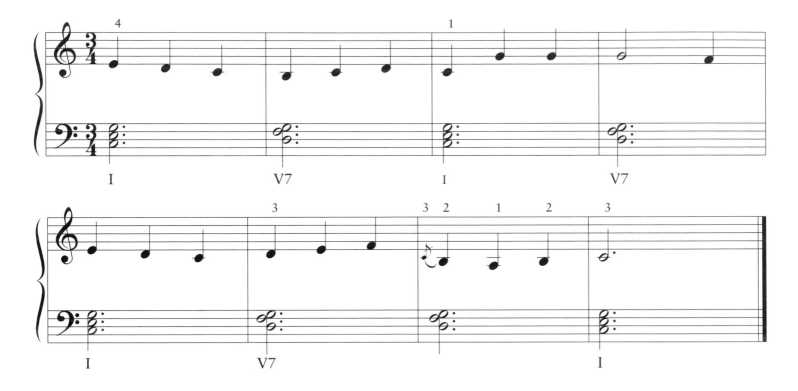

Arpeggios

Chords in the left hand can be varied by playing them as arpeggios, one note after another instead of all together.

Here is another miniature piece based on these two chords, this time used in arpeggio form.

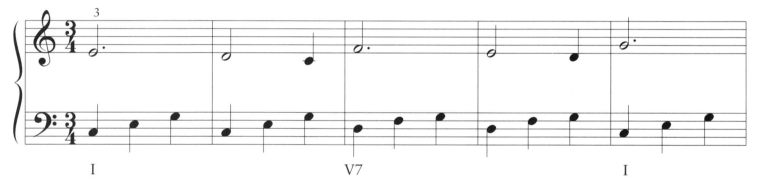

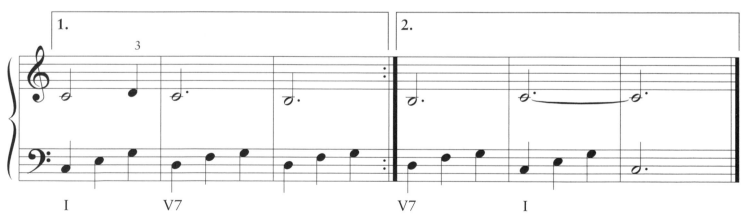

Here again you may find it a good idea to work a little on each hand before putting them together. Don't forget to observe the repeat sign with the first and second endings. The first time play it directly to the double bar repeat sign, and on the repetition, skip the three bars under figure 1, and go right on to the second ending under figure 2.

Rests

Now if you have learned the little piece, let us try a variation of it. Instead of adding notes, We shall leave out a few. Just as we learned to count notes for a certain number of beats, we must now learn to count *rests* which indicate that no note at all is to be sounded. A quarter rest looks like this (𝄽) and indicates silence for one beat; and as for the others. see the table.

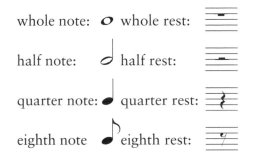

whole note:	𝅝	whole rest:	𝄻
half note:	𝅗𝅥	half rest:	𝄼
quarter note:	♩	quarter rest:	𝄽
eighth note	♪	eighth rest:	𝄾

Now let us vary the left hand of our piece by taking out some of the notes and substituting rests—see if you can learn to play it this way.

If you find the left hand a bit difficult practice it by itself until you get it, then add the right hand.

Do you prefer this version of the piece? It will be easier for the melody in the right hand to come through since there is no accompaniment on the first beat of each measure; as you gradually become a better pianist you will notice that your pieces sound better when you can make the melody sing out above the accompaniment. As you listen to recordings of great pianists, it is interesting to notice this point as a detail in their artistry. In your own playing, this is one of the things that you keep in mind to master; if you don't find it easy right now, be patient.

Would you like to try still one more variation of this little piece? Play the whole thing an octave higher, both the right hand and the left. (Perhaps you know now what an octave is—it is the distance of eight notes after which the same notes are repeated at a different level, either higher or lower.)

Here is how our piece looks at the higher octave. Now we will have to write both hands in the G clef (or *treble clef,* for the left hand will be moving up from middle C, and it would take too many leger lines to indicate it in the *bass clef* (𝄢). Of course, the right hand will now be in the higher register, and it is not easy to read it up there. But as long as you have learned it at the lower octave, it won't be difficult to just take it up an octave.

Perhaps you may prefer this version to the original one at the lower octave. Learn it as well as you can, and see if you can memorize it. With a little practice you may find that you can play it without having to look at the music anymore.

By the way, notice a few new indications that we have added. The tempo direction at the very beginning, *allegretto,* means moderately fast; *crescendo* means get louder; and *diminuendo* means get softer. *Crescendo* is often abbreviated *cresc.,* and *diminuendo, dim.*—and even more often these directions are indicated by the symbols, ⟨ and ⟩.

Some Performance Directions

Allegro .... fast
Allegretto .... moderately fast
Moderato .... moderate speed
Andante .... rather slow
Adagio .... very slow
f or forte .... loud
ff or fortissimo .... very loud
p or piano .... soft
pp or pianissimo .... very soft

As for the letters *p*, *f*, and *pp* they are abbreviations of the Italian words *piano, forte,* and *pianissimo* meaning soft, loud and very soft.

The direction *ritardando* at the end means that you can slow down the speed or tempo a little. Sometimes pianists do this at the end of a piece even when it's not indicated in the music. In certain cases this may be an inexcusable liberty while in others it may be entirely appropriate. There is a very large area in the performance of any music that just has to be left to the discretion of the performer. As you continue to develop as a pianist, your own musical taste will continue to mature.

Suggestions for Practice

It may take a good deal of practice to learn the new piece in this lesson to your satisfaction—but be patient, and you will get it little by little.

Remember that working with the hands separately is most helpful in learning a new and difficult piece, so take the time to do this at the beginning. When you first put the hands together, do it particularly slowly at first, later increasing the tempo as you get to know it better.

It may also he helpful to isolate any passage that gives you special trouble, and practice it by itself, later on fitting it into the rest of the piece.

And of course, as always, he sure to begin each practice session with your five-finger exercises, and review some of your old pieces every day.

A Little Technical Work

By now we have covered a great deal of ground, and soon we shall go on to new things, such as playing melodies that go beyond the range of a five-finger hand position. But before we do, it might be a good idea to pause for breath and take time out to practice some exercises

In or first lesson we had a very simple five-finger exercise in five notes from C to G in quarter notes, and there is no reason why you can't do this exercise every day with all the work we've had by now, though, you may be able to do it a little faster, so let us try it now in eighth notes instead of quarter notes.

And don't forget the left hand too, an octave lower.

And of course you can try it with both hands.

If you'd like to vary this exercise, limit the number of notes to three, which will give you the opportunity of playing it with different sets of fingers.

Now we have a three-finger exercise if you have tried it with the first, second, and third fingers you will have found that it is not at all difficult. Try it now with the second, third, and fourth fingers.

This is a little harder, but now see if you can do it with the weakest fingers of all, the third, fourth, and fifth.

This actually is quite difficult, and you had better practice it slowly at first. But these fingers always need strengthening, so the more practice you can give it, the better. Do it very slowly and strongly and firmly, almost exaggerating the finger action.

Let us try these exercises with the left hand too. You might start by varying our five-finger exercise to start with the thumb on middle C, going down to F as follows.

Now try the little three-finger exercise, beginning on middle C and going down to A, and again do it with the three possible sets of fingering that we have used in the right hand, the first, second, and third; the second, third, and fourth; and finally the most difficult, the third, fourth, and fifth.

These exercises, quite frankly, are not too interesting musically; but for the pianist they are exactly what the punching bag is for the boxer, or the exercises at the barre for the dancer, a necessary and inevitable discipline that is required in order to advance to higher levels. So be patient and spend at least a few minutes of your time at the piano warming up with these exercises—not all of them at one time, of course, but as much as you think you can profit from.

Don't forget that playing the piano, after all, is a physical activity which will only be mastered if you give it the necessary time and work. With these exercises, you will have the satisfaction of knowing that eventually they will make it possible for you to do wonderful things at the piano. This book, after all, is only a two-dimensional outline—you have to add the third dimension of time and practice to make it come to life.

Scales

So far, we have confined ourselves to melodies that can be played by the five fingers in a fixed position, occasionally with a slight extension for an extra note or two. But this simple approach will not serve for everything as we advance beyond this rather limited range.

If, for example, you play a complete *scale*—going up step by step from middle C to C an octave higher—you will find that you run into trouble.

Of course it would be very easy to divide the scale between the hands as follows.

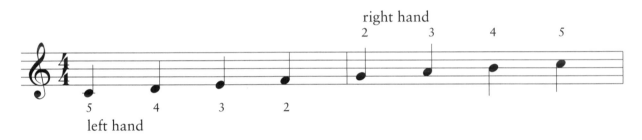

But what if the left hand is busy with an accompaniment, and you want to play this scale with the right hand alone?

Fortunately there is a little trick that makes it possible, and that you will find immensely useful as you go on to do more difficult things. It is called "putting the thumb under," and if you try it you will find that it is not at all difficult.

Start by playing the first three notes of the scale—C, D, and E, with the first, second, and third fingers of the right hand—and while you keep holding the third finger down on F, shift the thumb from its original position on C to the note F above your third finger. Now you're ready to continue all the way up to high C without any further trouble.

Here is the scale on C, written with this fingering.

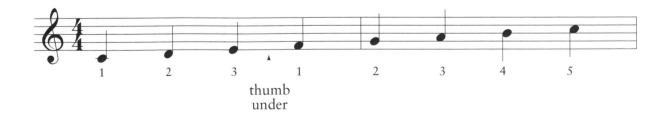

The trick of putting the thumb under is so important that it will be worth taking the time to do a few extra finger exercises to accustom ourselves to this technique.

For a moment review the three-finger exercise that we had in the last lesson.

Now substitute the thumb for the third finger on E by putting it under the hand as we have just learned to do. Here is the new fingering for this exercise.

That's not very difficult, as you see.

Now extend it a step, and make it an exercise of four notes, going from C to F. In this case, we will play E with the third finger, and cross the thumb under it at this point to play the note E. Here is the new version of the exercise.

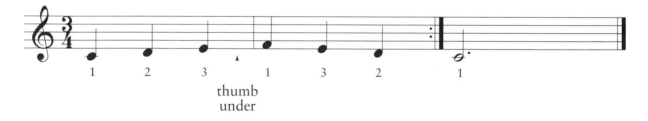

To make this exercise work more easily, get into the habit of moving the thumb to its new position just as soon as you can after you finish playing middle C. Now with a little practice on our new exercise, you will find it much easier to go back to our scale on C with the correct fingering of crossing the thumb under. Do it a few times in succession for practice, and finish with an octave skip from middle C to high C.

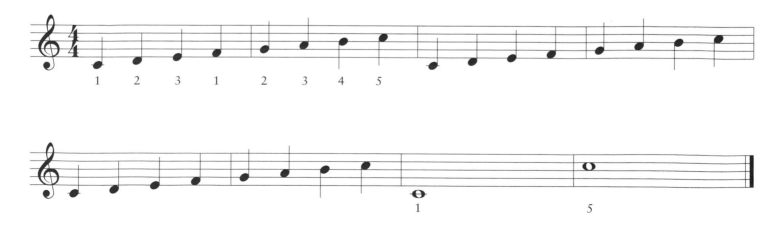

Now that you have arrived at high C, you will find that it is easy to come down the scale by a process called "crossing the hand over." Play the scale going down from high C until you reach F with your thumb. Then, while holding the thumb on F, cross the hand over the thumb so that you can play the E below with the third finger. This will carry you down to D with the second finger, and C with the thumb to complete the descending scale. Here, then, is the scale going down, with the correct fingering cross.

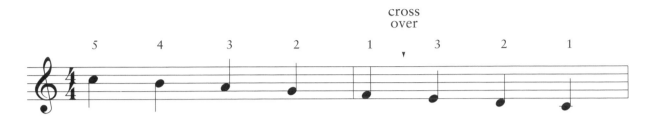

If you find you can do that without too much difficulty, then make a little exercise by going up and down the scale a few times in succession as follows.

As with all your exercises, this will benefit you the most if you play it strongly and firmly, keeping a very good hand position.

Now before going ahead any further with the right hand, we must apply what we know to the left hand too. Start on middle C with the thumb and go down to A with the third finger. Then, while holding A, put the thumb under to play G, and finish the scale down to low C as follows.

Just as we did with the right hand, let us try the exercises for putting the thumb under, first with three notes, and then with four.

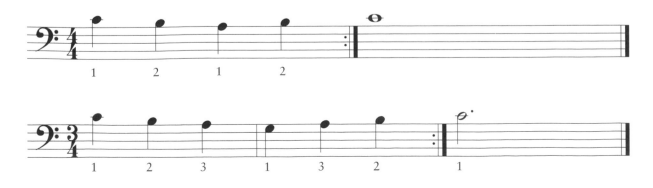

Play the entire scale of C, going down an octave, a few times, and finish with the octave skip from middle C to low C.

And now, just as we did with the right hand, reverse the scale. Start with low C this time, and go up an octave by "crossing the hand over" when you get to the thumb on G. Finish with the third finger on A, the second finger on B. and the thumb on middle C, as follows.

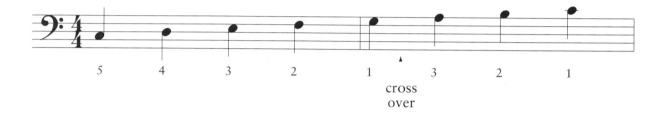

Finally, play the scale going up and then down a few times in succession.

If you'd like to play the scales with the hands together an octave apart, you may find it a little difficult just now, since the hands reverse themselves as far as fingering is concerned, and this makes for a little problem in coordination. But you certainly won't have any difficulty if you play the hands going in opposite directions. Start both hands with the thumbs on middle C, and then play the right hand an octave up and the left hand an octave down, and then return to middle C. You will have the same fingering in both hands, so you can save time by practicing both hands at once.

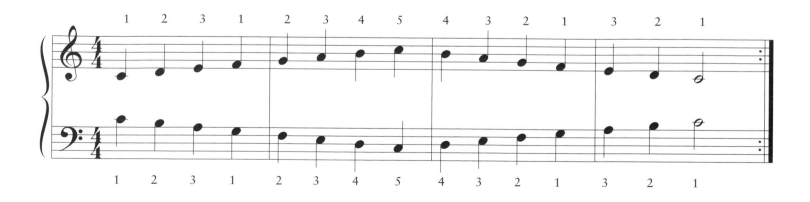

If you want to vary this, you can move the right hand up an octave, or the left hand down an octave, thus avoiding a collision on middle C. As usual, practice strongly and firmly, with a very good hand position. There are a few dissonances when you play the scales in opposite directions, and your neighbors may not like it, but it will help make a pianist out of you.

Suggestions for Practice

Scales form one of the most valuable additions to the technical exercises with which you begin each practice session—make the best use of them. The trick of putting the thumb under is a necessary technical tool for advancing to more difficult things, so practice it patiently and assiduously!

Continue to review your old pieces. If you have any other method books, you can go ahead with them on your own. Use your judgment as to how far you can go, and how much new material you can profitably take. As general rule, it is better to do less, but to do it well.

Epilogue

One of the most valuable things you can derive from working at the piano—even if you never get to be an expert performer—is a heightened awareness of the skill and beauty of other pianists' playing. You can attend a piano recital now and appreciate it in a way that you never could have if you hadn't learned a little about playing the piano yourself. Actually, a recital by a great pianist can be among the memorable experiences of your life, and you should take the opportunity of hearing good pianists whenever you can.

Go to as many concerts as you can, listen to as many records as you can, and learn what you can from pianists who are better than you. But always remember that there is no substitute for the joy of making music yourself.

If you have mastered this book on your own, you have accomplished a great deal, even though you have only just begun to scratch the surface! By now, if you have not already found one, you must look for a teacher who is well qualified and sympathetic to you. As you continue to work and improve, you will find that the pleasure that music can bring to you is limitless.